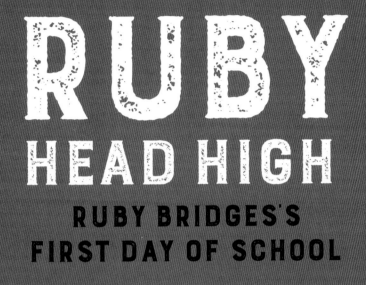

RUBY
HEAD HIGH
RUBY BRIDGES'S
FIRST DAY OF SCHOOL

Irène Cohen-Janca

Illustrated by Marc Daniau

Creative Editions

• • •

This story was inspired by the painting
The Problem We All Live With, by Norman Rockwell,
reinterpreted in this book by illustrator Marc Daniau.
The editors warmly thank Norman Rockwell's rights holders.

• • •

Ruby tête haute by Irène Cohen-Janca and Marc Daniau, copyright © 2017, Les Éditions des Éléphants.
Translation copyright © 2019, The Creative Company. Additional illustrations © 2019 Marc Daniau.
This edition was published by arrangement with The Picture Book Agency, France. All rights reserved.
Artwork on p. 32 Approved by and Courtesy of the Norman Rockwell Family Agency:
Norman Rockwell Museum (1864–1978), *The Problem We All Live With*, Illustration for *Look*, January 14, 1964.
Norman Rockwell Museum Collection, Stockbridge, MA.
Photo of Ruby Bridges: Getty Images (Bettmann) • Translated from the French and edited by Amy Novesky
Designed by Rita Marshall • Published in 2019 by Creative Editions • P.O. Box 227, Mankato, MN 56002 USA
Creative Editions is an imprint of The Creative Company www.thecreativecompany.us • All rights reserved.
No part of the contents of this book may be reproduced by any means without the written permission of the
publisher. • Printed in China • **Library of Congress Cataloging-in-Publication Data** • Names: Daniau, Marc,
illustrator. Title: Ruby, Head High / illustrated by Marc Daniau. • Summary: Inspired by an iconic
Norman Rockwell painting and translated from an original French text, this is a story about the day a
little girl held her head high and changed the world. • Identifiers: ISBN 978-1-56846-341-4
This title has been submitted for CIP processing under LCCN 2018019508.

The painting of the little black girl in the white dress was on the easel when we entered the classroom. Our teacher asked us what we thought of it.

Louise immediately raised her hand. "She has rich parents. They are afraid she will be kidnapped, so she is protected by the police!"

"I think she made a mistake and they are taking her to prison," Nadia said.

Lucien had another idea. "She does not want to go to school, so the police are forcing her to go."

We all laughed because we knew Lucien hated school and preferred to hang out on the street. The teacher asked for calm. Then she asked me. "What do you think, Nora?"

I was sure the adults around her were there to protect her from danger, but I was too shy to say what I thought.

I thought about the little girl in the painting all day. And that night I dreamed of her. She told me her story. . . .

My name is Ruby Bridges. I grew up in Louisiana, a state of fantastic, alligator-filled swamps, deep dark forests, tropical flowers, and lots and lots of birds. The Mississippi River flows, mighty and terrible, quiet as a stream, and cities rise from where swamps used to be.

• • •

Louisiana is also a state where black people are kept separate from white people. This is called segregation.

It took a lot of time and trouble before things started to change. New laws banned segregation. Still, many whites refused to live with blacks. Only white children were allowed to go to the neighborhood school. My school was far from our house.

· · ·

It was 1960, and I was six years old.

We did not have a lot of money, but we had a lot of joy.

. . .

My mom loved to cook—rice and catfish, banana pudding, cake—so many good things that scented the whole house.

. . .

After school, I played knucklebones with my friends, skipped rope, climbed trees.

. . .

In the summer, a band of us—my brothers and sisters and my many cousins—all went to my grandparents' farm. We didn't have much time to wander or get bored. We had to harvest and can vegetables. In the evenings, we fell into bed exhausted.

. . .

I was a happy girl. And then everything changed.

One day, there was a loud knock at the door. People who had been fighting for equal rights told my parents that black children had the right to attend white schools. They just needed to pass an exam. My father shut the door. He did not believe there would ever be equality. But my mother believed in fighting. She convinced my father to let me take the exam.

• • •

More than one hundred children took the test. Only six girls passed. I was one of them.

• • •

I was told it would take courage and strength to attend my new school. I did not understand why it took courage and strength. All I knew is that I would miss my friends. I wasn't happy about that.

On the first day of school, I put on my best dress, and my mother carefully braided my hair.

. . .

Four police officers waited outside our house. They told us they would take us.

. . .

A large crowd was gathered outside William Frantz Public School. The din of the sirens and shouts reminded me of Mardi Gras. But this was no carnival.

My mother and I waited all day in the school office. A big clock hung on the wall. All day, angry white parents came and left with their children. At three o'clock, we were told to leave.

• • •

Outside, the crowd had grown even bigger. People waved signs, and children chanted rhymes:

    Two, four, six, eight, we don't want to integrate

    Eight, six, four, two, we don't want a chigeroo

• • •

One woman held a small coffin with a black baby doll in it, and that scared me more than anything. I did not understand what was happening.

• • •

The next day, when I arrived at school, the crowd was even bigger. Women with hateful faces screamed that they wanted to poison me.

A smiling white woman was waiting for me. She took my hand and opened the door of a quiet classroom and told me to take a seat. There were rows of desks and chairs, but no other children. It was just she and I.

• • •

Her name was Mrs. Henry, my new teacher. I loved her immediately. I learned to read and to write. I discovered mathematics, history, geography.

• • •

Slowly, the other children returned to school, but they went to separate classrooms, far from me. I could hear their laughter and screams.

• • •

One day, a little girl waved to me. I imagined playing knucklebones, jumping rope, climbing trees with her. But not today. Tomorrow, maybe.

Anger rumbled throughout the city. Riots erupted, and fires were lit to scare us. My grandparents lost the land they were renting, their farm. My father was fired from his job.

. . .

I didn't feel like eating anymore, not even my mother's rice and catfish, not even cake. At night, instead of dreams, I had nightmares.

. . .

My mother told me to pray even harder.

It was hard, but we were not alone. All of our neighbors checked on us. They protected us.

• • •

And we received letters of support from all over the country. One letter made my mother cry. It was from Mrs. Roosevelt, the wife of the former president of the United States.

• • •

The letters reminded us that we were courageous and that we were not alone.

The next day, I stopped in front of the angry crowd. I was not afraid.

• • •

Later, Mrs. Henry asked me what I said to them.

"I prayed."

Mrs. Henry smiled. I never forgot that smile.

• • •

In time, the angry crowd grew smaller. I was finally allowed to join the rest of the children at recess. I asked a little boy if I could play with him. He said no. His mother told him he could not play with me because I was black. Only, he used another word.

• • •

And that's when I understood why people were so angry at a little girl going to school.

I was black.

. . .

But by the next school year, the police and the crowds were gone. Instead there were lots of children—white and black.

. . .

When I entered the classroom, a new teacher was waiting for us.

"Where is Mrs. Henry?" I asked.

Nobody answered me. My heart was broken. I had lost my teacher and my friend. It was as if nothing had happened.

. . .

But I would never be the same.

From that day forward, I would not only fight to go to school, I would fight for an education. I would fight for all black children to have the same opportunities as white children. I would hold my head high.

I am Ruby Bridges. . . .

I would never be the same, either.

. . .

That night I dreamed of Ruby Bridges.

I dreamed of the painting my teacher shared at school, a little black girl in a white dress walking to school surrounded by federal marshals and angry protesters, but all alone.

. . .

Ruby no longer walked alone. I was right by her side. And instead of a sad gray wall, ugly words, and red stains, we were surrounded by beautiful trees, singing birds, a blue sky.

. . .

Ruby, head high, and I.

ABOUT RUBY

Ruby Bridges Hall is an American civil rights activist, philanthropist, and founder of The Ruby Bridges Foundation, which promotes the values of tolerance, respect, and appreciation of differences. She also serves on the board of the Norman Rockwell Museum.

ABOUT THE PAINTING

Ruby Bridges's historic walk took place six years after the 1954 United States Supreme Court Brown v. Board of Education *ruling declared that state laws establishing separate public schools for black and white students were unconstitutional, and represented a definite victory for the American Civil Rights Movement. Among those Americans to take note of the event was artist Norman Rockwell, a longtime supporter of the goals of equality and tolerance. In his early career, editorial policies governed the placement of minorities in his illustrations (restricting them to service industry positions only). However, in 1963, Rockwell confronted the issue of prejudice head-on with one of his most powerful paintings,* The Problem We All Live With. *Inspired by the story of Ruby Bridges and school integration, the image featured a young African American girl being escorted to school amidst signs of protest and fearful ignorance. The painting ushered in a new era in Rockwell's career, and remains an important national symbol of the struggle for racial equality.* —Norman Rockwell Museum

To commemorate the fiftieth anniversary of Ruby Bridges's historic first day of school integrating the William Frantz Public School in New Orleans on November 14, 1960, Norman Rockwell's painting, *The Problem We All Live With*, was placed on display at the White House in 2010, at the request of president Barack Obama, a powerful reminder of the little black girl in the white dress who changed history. The painting is in the collection of the Norman Rockwell Museum in Stockbridge, MA. Learn more at nrm.org.